**DON'T WASTE
YOUR SPORTS**

DON'T WASTE YOUR SPORTS

C.J. MAHANEY

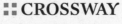

CROSSWAY

WHEATON, ILLINOIS

Don't Waste Your Sports

Copyright © 2011 by C.J. Mahaney

Published by Crossway
            1300 Crescent Street
            Wheaton, Illinois 60187

Cover design: Matthew Wahl

First printing 2010

Printed in the United States of America

Scripture quotations are from the ESV® Bible (*The Holy Bible,
English Standard Version®*), copyright © 2001 by Crossway.
Used by permission. All rights reserved.

Trade paperback ISBN: 978-1-4335-2247-5
PDF ISBN: 978-1-4335-2248-2
Mobipocket ISBN: 978-1-4335-2249-9
EPub ISBN: 978-1-4335-2250-5
12-pack ISBN: 978-1-4335-2575-9

Library of Congress Cataloging-in-Publication Data
Mahaney, C. J.
   Don't waste your sports / C. J. Mahaney.
      p.   cm.
   ISBN 978-1-4335-2247-5 (tpb)
   1. Sports—Religious aspects. 2. Athletes—Religious life.
3. Spirituality. I. Title.
GV706.42.M34   2010
796.01—dc22
                                    2010022865

Crossway is a publishing ministry of Good News Publishers.

VP		19	18	17	16	15	14	13	12	11	10
14	13	12	11	10	9	8	7	6	5	4	3	2	1

CONTENTS

HOW TO USE THIS BOOKLET

Athletes, this booklet is for you.

Parents and discussion leaders, this booklet is also for you. It's for anyone who wants to learn, or help others learn, about what it means to let a right knowledge of God shape the way we practice and play sports.

Application and discussion questions for athletes (useful whether you're reading this solo or leading a group discussion) are located at the back of the booklet (see page 47). Parents, you'll find a section addressed directly to you on page 49. It includes some thoughts on parenting and sports, as well as some application questions.

For more resources, visit www.dontwaste yoursports.com.

1

SPORTS AT THEIR BEST—AND WORST

I can see it clearly. My feet are firmly planted on the starting block, knees bent, arms hanging loosely at my sides. The water is still. I take a final deep breath, waiting for the gun to go off, anticipating my lunge into the pool.

It takes little imagination to relive this moment. I can't count the number of times I dove into the pool, absolutely intent on winning.

What led me to compete as a swimmer? Well, at first my parents made me do it. They put me on the swim team when I was six. And let's be clear—I despised every moment of it, because swimming is pure and monotonous discipline. And I wasn't disciplined. I was a born loafer.

Here's the strange thing: I continued to swim until college, and in spite of my hatred for early morning practices and frigid pools, at every meet I was driven to win. I was elated when I won and depressed when I lost (which was, sadly, much more frequent). I despised swimming. So what explanation is there for my passion to win?

At the time I would have said I was competitive.

What I didn't perceive then was my own passion to be admired. Swimming was merely my stage, my opportunity to impress others with my athleticism. Each event was a platform for drawing attention to myself. And it was no different in the other sports I played (and liked better): baseball, basketball, football. Now, as I reflect on those years, I see more clearly what was in my heart as a young man. I can see how proud I was.

The problem wasn't swimming, or baseball, basketball, or football. These and other sports are gifts from God, and competing in them can and should be a joy. I love playing a variety of sports in the backyard with my son and grandsons. I play golf (which, for me, is a means of cultivating humility). I keep two gloves and a ball in my office, and I play catch in the parking lot so often the UPS guy probably wonders whether I actually work. My family's holiday traditions include a football game the day after Thanksgiving. Everyone plays. Even the ladies. My wife and three daughters play, regardless of cold weather, muddy fields, even pregnancy. (Although I'll admit the game gets shorter every year.)

Sports are a gift from God. But as soon as you introduce the human heart, things get complicated.

Why is it that sports seem to bring out the best and the worst in us? Sports can provide hours of happiness, but they can also ignite impatience, anger, even rage. What gives?

If you've ever asked yourself this question, you're not alone. Erik Thoennes, a professor and former college football player, puts it this way:

> I had the delightful experience this week of watching a dozen five-year-old children get

a tennis lesson. They were asked by their instructor to simply run forward and then backward over a ten foot span. They did far more than run. Skipping, leaping, bounding, hopping, spinning, laughing, animal imitations, running with closed eyes, dramatically falling, jumping up again, and purposely crashing into one another, all became part of the lesson. When the instructor armed the children with racquets, the fun really began. The racquets quickly became guitars, swords, canes, horses, trombones, rifles, and fishing poles. The lesson continually bordered on becoming "unproductive" and utter chaos because playing was as instinctual to the children as breathing. The teacher was successful because he appreciated the children's insatiable need to play, and allowed for copious amounts of it within his instruction.

But it's not always like that. Dr. Thoennes points out the dark side of sports:

This week I also read of a father who went to jail for eight years for unintentionally killing one of his son's tennis opponents after drugging the opponent with medication that causes drowsiness. The father, who was doing all he could to ensure the athletic "success" of his son and daughter, had similarly spiked the water bottles of twenty-seven other rivals over a three year period. The difference between the fun loving instructor and the winning obsessed father could not be more pronounced. And their differences highlight drastically different ways of viewing sport in Western culture. . . . One appreciates the actual process of playing a sport; the other has sadly turned sport into an ugly expression of human pride, . . . envy, and malice. What will keep us from turning sport into something ugly rather than beautiful?[1]

Good question.

Sports, at their best, *are* beautiful. In a 2008 game, Western Oregon University softball player Sara Tucholsky hit a three-run home run to give her team the lead, but while trying to touch first base she tore her ACL and collapsed.

---

[1]K. Erik Thoennes, "Created to Play: Thoughts on Play, Sport, and the Christian Life" (paper presented at the Evangelical Theological Society Annual Meeting, Providence, RI, November 2008).

The rules prohibited her teammates from helping her round the bases. That's when two of her opponents—including Mallory Holtman, the conference's all-time leading home run hitter—lifted Tucholsky and carried her around the base path all the way to home plate.

But we've all seen sports turn ugly, too. Maybe you don't know anyone who drugged his opponents' water bottles. But turn on ESPN, and on any given night you'll hear about steroids, suspensions, and scandals.

So how do we keep sports beautiful? Does God care either way? What are sports all about anyway?

This booklet exists to answer these important questions. My prayer is that by the time we're done, we'll discover answers from the wisdom of God's Word. We'll find real guidance for athletes in the pages of Scripture. We'll see that sports, although they bring us great joy, are not actually about us at all. Something—and Someone—much more important is in view.

2
WHAT ARE SPORTS REALLY FOR?

You won't find track meets or golf tournaments in the pages of Scripture. But we're about to look at a passage that applies to all of life, including sports. These few words, if by the grace of God we understand and obey them, will transform our lives.

Are you ready for this? It's a familiar passage, but perhaps you haven't applied it to the playing field:

> So, whether you eat or drink, or whatever you do, do all to the glory of God. (1 Cor. 10:31)

This simple sentence is loaded with divine wisdom for every part of our sports, from practices to playoffs. So few words, so much wisdom.

We'll grasp it more easily if we know who it was written to and why. So we're taking a short detour from the world of sports to the world of first-century Greece. (Trust me, we'll be back to sports in a minute.)

First Corinthians 10:31 is part of a letter from the apostle Paul to Christians in the city of Corinth. They had asked whether it was okay for Christians to eat food that had been sacrificed to idols and then sold in the market (1 Cor. 8:1–10:33). In other words, were they allowed to enjoy a steak dinner if the beef had been offered as a religious sacrifice to an idol?

This may not sound like a big deal to us, but for Christians in Corinth it was a very big deal. Their culture was full of idol worship. So the question of whether you could eat food that had been offered to idols was starting serious arguments in the church.

In response to their question, Paul explained that the food itself wasn't damaged by the idolatrous sacrifice, and Christians weren't harmed if they ate it. However, Paul does tell them not to attend pagan banquets. Why? Because for Christians to attend these popular events was to associate with the worship of demons. Attending these banquets was out of the question.

Here's Paul's point: the important thing for the Corinthians was not the origin of their food, but the nature of their worship. "Therefore," he tells them, "flee from idolatry" (1 Cor. 10:14). Then he says, "Whether you eat or drink, or whatever you do, do all to the glory of God" (1 Cor. 10:31).

With this background, we can understand that 1 Corinthians 10:31 is calling us to do two things:

- examine our hearts and lives for the presence of idolatry, and
- devote ourselves to the glory of God in all of life, including sports.

These two principles have a lot to say about our participation in sports. They also make a surprising promise: sports, like anything else in life, is an opportunity for us to glorify God.

That's right. Sports, just like those Corinthian steak dinners, are a gift from God. From swimming to softball, wrestling to rugby, baseball to basketball, cross-country running, gymnastics, hockey, decathlons, karate, track, golf, football, tennis, lacrosse—the list could go on. Each of them is a gift from a gracious God. Each, when enjoyed properly, can glorify God.

We have to be careful, though, because this promise carries a warning label, too. If it's possible to use sports for God's glory, then there is also a way to misuse sports for our own glory. And that is exactly what the sinful heart—mine and yours included—is often all too eager to do.

We'll talk about examining our lives for the presence of idolatry a little later in this booklet. But first let's consider an important question: how do we glorify God—and not ourselves—in our sports?

To answer that, we need to know who God is and what brings him glory.

3

MEETING GOD BEFORE THE OPENING TIP

Using sports to glorify someone is not a new idea.

You may already know that the athletic brand Nike is named after the ancient Greek goddess of victory. But perhaps you didn't know that the original Olympic Games—which occurred hundreds of years before Christ was born—was an athletic festival held in honor of the Greek god Zeus. On the central day of the festival, one hundred oxen were sacrificed to him. (This rivals modern Super Bowls for the most absurd halftime show in the history of sports.)

Whether we use sports to glorify a pagan god named Zeus, a gifted professional like LeBron James, or ourselves, we distort and mis-use sports.

If we don't know who God really is, we'll

seek our own glory instead of his. We'll give glory to the created instead of the Creator. We'll rob God of the glory that only he deserves. We'll waste our sports.

So we must first get to know the true God of all creation—including sports. Who is he? What do we mean by his "glory"?

Now, if you're wondering what all this has to do with your jump shot, we're getting there soon. Hang with me. It's like with any sport—you've got to know how to run the plays before you go out and run the plays. You've got to understand the West Coast offense before you can run it. You've got to understand the full-court press before you can execute it. In the same way, we've got to study God's character before we move on to the practical stuff. This isn't just for scholars (who normally don't have game). If you're a Christian athlete, you must study theology and not just the playbook.

When we think about who God is, we need help. We have small brains and an infinite God. We're jumping into the deep end of the theological pool. So I've enlisted a smart guy to help

us out, a theologian named J. I. Packer. Here's
how he describes the God who gave us sports:

> Our personal life is a finite thing: it is lim-
> ited in every direction, in space, in time,
> in knowledge, in power. But God is not so
> limited. He is eternal, infinite and almighty.
> He has us in his hands; we never have him in
> ours. Like us, he is personal; but unlike us,
> he is *great*. . . . The Bible never lets us lose
> sight of [God's] majesty and his unlimited
> dominion over all his creatures.[2]

Let's look at J. I. Packer's statement again
in slo-mo:

- **God is eternal:** When it comes to his age,
  God has no beginning and he has no end.
  He cannot be outlived (Ps. 90:2; 102:25–
  27).
- **God is infinite:** When it comes to physical limitations, God has, well, none. He is
  equally present everywhere. We can never
  go to a place where he is not (Jer. 23:23–
  24; Ps. 139:7–12).

---

[2] J. I. Packer, *Knowing God* (Downers Grove, IL: InterVarsity, 1973), 83.

- **God is almighty:** When it comes to his strength, God defeats all obstacles and all enemies. He accomplishes whatever he pleases (Gen. 18:14; Ps. 115:3; Matt. 19:26).

Amazingly, though, God doesn't just list these jaw-dropping stats about himself. He shows us his glory most clearly in the person of his Son. In another letter to the Corinthians, Paul puts it this way:

> God, who said, "Let light shine out of darkness," has shone in our hearts to give the light of the knowledge of the glory of God in the face of Jesus Christ. (2 Cor. 4:6)

This is incredible. The God who spoke light and time into existence shows us his glory first and foremost in one person: Jesus Christ.

Why? Because in his death on the cross for our sins, Jesus bore the penalty for every time we have exalted ourselves instead of him, every angry word we've muttered at a referee, every complaint when our coach didn't put us in the game. He is our best glimpse of our eternal, infinite, and almighty God. And he is our only hope for the forgiveness of sins—forgiveness we need so desperately. As sinners, you and I have only one hope: Jesus Christ.

This is the eternal, almighty, infinite, and merciful God whose glory should be our passion and priority every time we step onto the field.

What does this have to do with my jump shot? Good question. We'll look at the answer on the next few pages.

4

PLAY TO THE GLORY OF GOD

Here's the difference knowing God makes: when I encounter the eternal, almighty, infinite, and merciful God, something changes in my heart. My attention turns away from myself and toward this glorious God. I walk onto the field much less likely to brag, jockey for attention, or try to win others' admiration. Every play, every inning, every race becomes an opportunity to draw attention to God.

That's what we call worship. And this is why worshiping God isn't just something we do in church. It's something we do in all of life, including our sports.

So 1 Corinthians 10:31 tells us something very important about our sports. Here's what this verse says to us:

> To bring glory to God as athletes, we play sports in a way that draws attention to God's greatness instead of our own.

This involves much more than kneeling in the end zone or pointing to the sky. You see, too often Christian athletes participate in sports without understanding the potential sports have for God's glory. We let culture, rather than Scripture, define our priorities and passions. We're all vulnerable to this. Here are some sure signs of misdirected priorities:

- We have no higher purpose than winning.
- We are more concerned about improving athletic skill than growing in godliness.
- We use sports to glorify ourselves, rather than glorifying God through godly actions.

Sadly, it is possible to devote massive amounts of time to sports while failing to grow in humility, perseverance, self-control, diligence, and other qualities appropriate to a follower of Christ. But if you search Scripture for what it says is truly important, you won't find athletic gifting, personal stats, championship trophies, or even a win-loss column. Scripture's emphasis is clearly on the glory of God, as revealed in the gospel, and on our imitation of his character. As Christians, we must adopt Scripture's priorities.

This is not to say that athletic skill doesn't matter. It is important. But it's not *most* important. Playing sports to the glory of God must be primary; athletic ability and achievements must be secondary. And that means every time we step onto the field, our priority will be to worship God, apply the gospel to our hearts, and become more like Christ.

What does this actually look like? What does it mean to worship God and imitate Christ at tip-off, at halftime, in the fourth inning or the fourth quarter? What does it look like when my team is way ahead—or way behind?

This is where things get very practical. We've studied the plays; now we're going to run them. We're moving from the locker room to the playing field. Ready?

THE GRATEFUL ATHLETE

First, we play to the glory of God by thanking him for his gifts.

Sports, and the ability to play them, are

gifts from a merciful God. They are part of God's kind design for humanity. In addition to being just plain fun, sports bring us many benefits, none of which we deserve. And we should thank God for all of them. Here are just a few:

Rest and Refreshment

In a fallen world, in the work and weariness of daily life, God has kindly given us sports and recreation to refresh us. He has built a wonderful rhythm into this world: work, rest; work, rest; work, rest. For some, sports are work; but for most of us, sports are part of God's gift of rest. And if we are paying attention, sports remind us of the eternal rest in God's presence that awaits all who trust in Christ and his death on the cross for forgiveness of sins.

Health

The physical and mental benefits of physical exercise are undeniable—and if we're going to exercise, sports are way more fun than the gym. Even a non-sport (in my opinion) like ultimate Frisbee is more enjoyable than just working out. Look at it this way: you could run on the treadmill, like I do, and despise every second of it, like I do. Or you could play an intense game of pick-up basketball.

Joy

Another obvious benefit of playing any sport is the sheer enjoyment of it. There's the perfectly executed soccer pass. In baseball, the line drive single into center field. The nasty junk ball that defies physics, freezes the batter, and plummets into the catcher's mitt for a strike. The volleyball spike. The golf drive down the middle of the fairway. The flawless twenty-foot putt for birdie. We are talking serious fun.

You can even find joy in just watching sports, whether it's someone you know or someone you don't. I love watching my son, Chad, play soccer. And there are many gifted professional athletes whom it is a joy to watch. Even though some athletes aren't aware that their gifts come from God, we can still appreciate their gifts and enjoy watching them display their talents.

These gifts of rest, health, and joy aren't

given merely for our own pleasure. They have a greater purpose: to reveal the greatness and graciousness of God. All of God's gifts—including a three-point shot and a volleyball spike—point away from themselves and back to God. They are intended to create fresh gratefulness to him and new affection for him.

When you were a child and received a birthday present, your parents might have taught you to first open the card and thank the giver, then unwrap the gift. They wanted you to understand that the gift doesn't reinforce selfishness; it draws attention to the giver.

The same is true with God. Each day we receive innumerable gifts from God, and each one points our attention to him. But how often do I go through my day tearing the wrapping paper off one gift after another, never pausing to read the card? How often do I disregard God while enjoying his gifts?

Every day.

Each of us tends to receive gifts from God without thanking him. We neglect the Giver rather than glorifying him.

Not thanking God seems like no big deal. But in fact the Bible teaches us that ingratitude is a sin. It's an insult to the God who showers us with good gifts.

So before your next practice or game, pause for a moment. Take time to thank God for this gift, for your health, for the weather—the list could go on and on.

Giving thanks to God for sports glorifies God. It also protects us from moving ourselves into the spotlight. If I'm not thanking God, I become big and God becomes small in my mind. But when we thank him for his gifts, we are humbly acknowledging that "from him and through him and to him are all things. To him be glory forever. Amen" (Rom. 11:36).

Let's be grateful athletes.

THE HUMBLE ATHLETE

In addition to thanking God for sports, we glorify him by playing the game with humility. Sadly, this is one quality that's often lacking, particularly in professional sports, and more and more in sports at all levels. But here's an astonishing truth: humility gets God's attention.

In Isaiah 66 we read, "This is the one to whom I will look: he who is humble and contrite in spirit and trembles at my word" (v. 2). God is decisively drawn to the humble. The humble athlete is the one who draws God's attention, and in this sense, drawing his attention means also attracting his grace—his unmerited kindness. And whether you're a starter or reserve, whether you play varsity or JV, you are no exception.

So how is humility expressed on the field? Here's a profile of the humble athlete:

The Humble Athlete Recognizes His Limitations

No athlete has unlimited skill. With two minutes remaining in a tied basketball game, you want the ball in the hands of Michael Jordan. In the bottom of the ninth in a tied baseball game, you'd be wise to bench Jordan and keep the bat out of his hands. Michael Jordan eventually discovered what we all must realize: none of us is universally gifted. We all come with divinely imposed limitations—limitations meant to humble us. Former college basketball player Pat Conroy got this. In his book *My Losing Season*, he humbly acknowledged, "I was born to be a point guard, but not a very good one."[3] That's the kind of humility we're talking about.

The Humble Athlete Welcomes Critique and Correction from Coaches and Teammates

No one enjoys being corrected. But if we're humble, we realize that we have weaknesses, so we welcome correction. If we're humble, we know we need to improve, so we want others to show us where and how. The proud athlete, on the other hand, will have none of this. He reacts to correction rather than welcoming it. He is easily offended.

The Humble Athlete Acknowledges the Contributions of Others

No athlete accomplishes anything alone. Any achievement is a group effort. A humble athlete

---

[3]Pat Conroy, *My Losing Season: A Memoir* (New York: Bantam Dell/ Random House, 2003), 1.

who scores doesn't dance in the end zone by himself as if no one else was involved in the play. Instead, he acknowledges that his team made the score possible.

My son, Chad, loves soccer. He introduced me to it and now I love soccer. We enjoy watching matches in the European league and the World Cup. But there is something about soccer that I find very strange. When a player scores a goal, he runs as hard as he can away from his teammates, who then run as fast as they can after him! The striker then retreats to a corner of the field, by himself, to receive the crowd's applause. This tradition is not just odd. It's ugly. This looks like nothing more than pride in action. This is not how a humble athlete glorifies God.

Instead, a humble athlete, if he scores, runs *to* his teammates and says, "I want to make something very clear: apart from all you did on defense and in passing, this score doesn't happen." The humble athlete sees that self-exaltation in team sports is absurd.

The Humble Athlete is Gracious in Defeat and Modest in Victory

For most of us, losing is inevitable. Losing with a proud attitude isn't. When the humble athlete loses, he is gracious. He recognizes that his opponents played better, and he sincerely congratulates them on their win. And when the humble athlete wins, he is modest. There are no excessive celebrations, no inappropriate victory dances. He realizes that victory is a gift from God and is an opportunity to draw attention to God, not himself. Win or lose, humility is always the appropriate response.

The Humble Athlete Honors His Coach

Think about it—your coach sacrificially gives his time and energy so you can be a better player. And if he's like most coaches, he doesn't even get paid for it. So if you're humble, you'll express gratitude—out loud—for the time your coach invests in your team. The humble athlete doesn't rip the coach in private. If he disagrees with the coach, he discusses it with him respectfully. The humble athlete accepts the role the coach chooses for him. When the humble athlete isn't playing, he doesn't slouch on the bench, muttering complaints; he cheers for his teammates on the field. And after every practice and every game, he thanks the coach for what he's done.

The Humble Athlete Respects Officials

A humble athlete doesn't protest a call—even if it was inaccurate. So when the referee blows a call, how will you respond? Will you demand a review? Will you roll your eyes? Mumble an insult? Or will you humbly accept the call?

The Humble Athlete Gives Glory for All His Athletic Accomplishments to God

He knows that all of his athletic skill, every point he scores, and every match he wins are ultimately gifts from God. What do we have that we have not received? Nothing. So the humble athlete transfers all the glory to God for all of his success.

Let's be humble athletes.

THE SERVANT ATHLETE

Remember what we said earlier about God's glory being displayed in Jesus Christ? Well here is something that should blow our minds. Scripture says that Jesus, even though he was God, "made himself nothing, taking the form of a servant" (Phil. 2:7).

Athletes, this is your example to follow. Whether you're the star player or the ball boy, team captain or the last substitute, you can glorify God by finding ways to serve others. Here are some ideas:

Encourage Your Teammates

If you're looking to serve your teammates, you'll want to see them improve and succeed. Notice your teammates' contributions—including the ones that don't show up on the stat sheet—and thank them. And when your teammate botches a play, help him improve without insulting him for the error.

Put the Team's Interest ahead of Your Own

Whenever you set aside personal preferences for the good of the team, that's serving. This may mean playing a position the coach has decided is best for the team, even if it's not the position you want. It may even mean not playing at all. It means playing defense as passionately and diligently as you play offense, and passing the ball instead of hogging it. It means asking the coach, "How can I best serve this team?"

Let's be servant-hearted athletes.

5
SPORTS IDOLS

We've been talking about how we can glorify God on the playing field—about how 1 Corinthians 10:31 applies to our sports. This passage of Scripture was written almost two thousand years ago. The apostle Paul was writing to people who were confused about eating steaks that had been offered as sacrifices to idols.

It sounds like another world, one hardly relevant to us or to sports. Does anyone worship idols today? If Paul were writing another letter and addressing it to us, do you ever wonder if he'd say something different?

I think he'd say exactly the same thing: "Whatever you do, do all to the glory of God." And I think he'd also tell us, as he told the Corinthians, to avoid idolatry.

Our world is different, yes. We're not usually thinking about pagan festivals or meat that was sacrificed to little statues. But our hearts are no different. We are tempted to make sports a much higher priority than they should be.

It's not hard to imagine Paul, if he wrote to us today, talking about what happens on playing fields and in front of TVs every weekend. Yep, sports. The temptation to idolatry isn't immediately obvious. You won't see people bowing down to statues or kneeling in little shrines before picking up the ball. But all around us, people are obsessed with sports. Athletes become celebrities. We memorize their stats, build our schedules around their games, make them our role models, and talk about almost nothing else. We exalt them. Our hearts bow down to our team, our sport, our victories. Worship is happening—on ESPN, and in our hearts.

That's why, just like the Corinthians, we need Scripture's sober warning. You see, if we're not playing sports to the glory of God, we're still worshiping—we're just worshiping someone or something else. And that's what the Bible calls idolatry.

So how do you know if sports are becoming an idol in your life? One way to tell is by examining your heart. Here are a few questions to ask yourself:

- Am I preoccupied with sports? Are they what I think about and talk about more than anything else?
- Are sports where my mind goes when I don't have anything else to think about?
- Are my most passionate conversations always about sports?
- Do I have an excessive passion for a particular team? Am I euphoric when they win, and depressed when they lose? For example, I grew up as a Redskins fan, and what happened in Sunday's game determined the mood in our home all week. That's idolatry. Disappointment is one thing; depression is another.
- Is my passion for a team, or for playing a particular sport, greater than my passion for Jesus Christ? For my family? For my church?

Another way to tell if sports have become an idol is to examine your time. Have sports taken the place in your schedule that belongs to other God-given priorities, like your family and your local church?

Yet another good way to tell if sports have become an idol is to examine your involvement in your church. When your church gathers, are you there? Or does the sports schedule trump the church calendar?

Now, missing an occasional Sunday meeting because of a sports event doesn't make you guilty of idolatry. What matters is your heart—what you love most. And what you love most usually shows up on your schedule. So if your life shows a consistent pattern of choosing sports events over gathering with God's people, I would encourage you to ask why. Has your heart been captured by the priority of the local church as taught in Scripture?

On the last day, when each of us gives account to God, you will have no regrets about appropriately limiting participation in sports so that you can be involved in your local church. No regrets at all.

6
YOUR NEXT GAME

My swimming career—along with every other sport I played—is a pathetic example of how *not* to play sports to the glory of God. As I look back, I now realize just how proud I was. The pool and the field were my stage, my opportunity to glorify myself—or at least try to. The countless swim meets and basketball, football, and baseball games were wasted opportunities. At every event, I wanted to be noticed. I wanted applause. Come to think of it, I wanted glory—the glory that belongs to God alone.

What about you? If you've played for your own glory rather than God's, is there hope?

Most definitely! But we won't find that hope in merely resolving to do better in the next game. When it comes to playing for the glory of God, "Just do it" doesn't cut it. There's no exercise program or set of drills that guarantees we won't waste our sports. That's because all of us, whether we're armchair athletes or seasoned pros, are sinners in need of a Savior. Left to ourselves, our hearts worship something other than God.

The only hope for every sinner—and that includes you and me—is found in the gospel: the glorious truth that "Christ died for our sins" (1 Cor. 15:3). In his death on the cross, Jesus Christ bore the penalty for every time we have exalted ourselves instead of him, every time we've idolized a sports team or an athlete, every time we've forgotten to thank God for his merciful gifts to us. We've wasted our sports. But in the grace of God through Christ, we can receive forgiveness.

This amazing grace also gives us hope for change. The cross of Christ not only makes possible forgiveness of sin, but also provides power to overcome sin.

I wish I had learned all of this as a young man. I had the opportunity to glorify God in my sports and I fumbled it. I wasted my sports.

You have the opportunity, by the grace of

God, not to waste yours. Your next game is an opportunity to glorify God.

I urge you: whatever you do—whether you play football or soccer, whether you're practicing or playing, whether you're in Little League or the pros, whether you win or lose—*whatever* you do, do all to the glory of God.

APPLICATION QUESTIONS FOR ATHLETES

1. The gospel is the center of what we believe as Christians. If someone asked you to explain the gospel, how would you explain it? What is the problem? What is the solution? (Hint: check out Romans 3:10–26 or 1 Corinthians 15:3–4.)

2. Does your passion for sports exceed your passion for the Savior, your church, or your family?

3. In an average week, how much time do you invest in sports, and how much time do you invest in reading Scripture and participating in your local church?

4. What is your plan for consistently reading and studying Scripture?

5. Is it possible to be both competitive and humble at the same time? How so?

6. It's easier to tear others down than build them up. What are some ways you currently encourage your teammates and your coach? If you don't, what are some ways to begin doing this?

7. Sports become ugly when we are jealous of another athlete's ability. What are some ways you are tempted to jealousy? Take time to think about ways you can encourage your teammates, especially the ones you might be tempted to be jealous of.

8. Has a coach ever pointed out something that helped you become a better athlete? What is the value in receiving feedback from those who could see your blind spots?

9. So you've read this booklet. Now step back and think of **one thing** you want to begin doing in the next practice or game. Write it on a piece of paper and keep the paper in your Bible. Pray for grace to grow in this area.

A WORD TO PARENTS

Parents, thank you for reading this booklet with your child. This is a humble act of leadership on your part.

In fact, every practice and every game is an opportunity to lead our children. Often, as parents, we think we have fulfilled our duty by simply attending our children's games and cheering. Not so! We are called to so much more. Informed by the gospel, we are called to lead our children wisely. Before the game, this includes preparing them to keep biblical priorities in mind while they play. After the game, this includes celebrating their expressions of godly character more than we celebrate their skill or the final score. Every moment our children spend in sports is a teaching moment.

Here are a few suggestions for parents, so that we don't waste our children's sports.

CELEBRATE GODLINESS

Our children will pursue what we applaud. They will emulate what we celebrate. If we celebrate scoring and winning, our children will define success in these terms. But if we celebrate evidences of godly character in our children, we will help them define success more biblically.

Sadly, if we don't lead our children, they may devote massive amounts of time to sports but fail to grow in godly character. We should celebrate qualities like humility, diligence, self-control, and perseverance in our children, whether they win or lose. Parents, you will be the difference-makers here.

So what do you encourage before a game? What do you celebrate after a game? Is it the spectacular plays? The score? The win? The stats? Or do you celebrate the displays of godliness by your child on the field?

PRIZE YOUR FAMILY

Over the years I've observed families in which the children played several sports apiece, and as a result, almost the only time the family spent together was as spectators at sporting events.

Parents, I encourage you to consider whether the majority of your family's time together is spent at sports events. If so, you may want to think about whether that time deepens and strengthens your family relationships. It might; it might not. This is why your leadership is so important.

And fathers, I'd be remiss if I didn't address you about a temptation that I'm familiar with in my own life: the tendency to devote excessive amounts of time to playing or watching sports, to the neglect of my family. So let me ask you—if someone looked at a typical week in your life, would they see that your family is your priority? Or would they see a significant amount of time used in playing or watching sports? (These are good questions for your wife to answer. She's probably more objective about your schedule than you are.)

LOVE YOUR LOCAL CHURCH

Missing an occasional Sunday meeting because of a sports event does not automatically mean that you're failing to lead your family. But what about the pattern? On the whole, what is the priority on your calendar—the local church, or athletics?

Parents, you have a unique calling to train your children to love and serve the local church.

If you and your family consistently miss your church's gatherings, you forfeit far more than you may realize. You forfeit the nearness of God that is experienced when the church gathers to worship him corporately. You forfeit an opportunity to hear from God through the preaching of his Word. You forfeit experiencing the countless gifts that God has distributed in the people around you. And you forfeit learning from the models of humility and servanthood that you find in the church. You don't want to give these up easily. You want to fight to maintain these priorities in your life and in your family!

On the last day, when each of us gives an account to God, you'll have no regrets about investing your family's time in your local church.

TRAINING FOR LIFE

Sports are a classroom for our children. Through sports we can teach our children to grow in godliness on the field. God has called you and equipped you to transfer biblical priorities to your children, and sports are one means to that end.

The time you invest into training your children to glorify God will bear fruit long after their days of playing competitive sports have concluded. And parents, these days will be over soon. Little League, JV, high school basketball—it all passes by so quickly. This is your opportunity. Don't waste it.

APPLICATION QUESTIONS FOR PARENTS

1. After a game, what are you more likely to celebrate: athletic skill and victories, or the display of godly character in your child's life?

2. What is one way your child currently displays godly character, and how can you identify and celebrate it?

3. What is one way your child could grow in godly character, and how can you encourage him or her to grow in this area?

4. Are there ways that sports distract you from your family? In what ways can you use sports to build your family together?

5. If someone were to study your life, which would they say you are more passionate about: playing and watching sports, or the Savior?

6. Is your family devoting so much time to sports that it hinders your involvement and service in your local church? If so, what are some changes that you can consider for the future?

7. Before your child's next practice or game, take time to pray with him or her and to thank God for all the benefits of sports. Remind your child that sports are a gift from God, the giver of all good gifts.

Personal Notes

Personal Notes

Personal Notes

Personal Notes

Personal Notes

Personal Notes